BawB's Raven Feathers
Reflections on the simple things in life

VOLUME I

Robert Chomany

INVERMERE PRESS • CALGARY, CANADA

Copyright © 2014, Robert Chomany

All rights reserved. No part of this publication may be reproduced or transmitted in any form or by any means, electronic or mechanical, including photocopying, recording, or any information storage and retrieval system without permission in writing from the author.

ISBN 978-0-9918821-5-1 (v. 1 : softcover)

Illustration: Jessee Wise
Book Design: Fiona Raven Book Design
Chief Editor: Rachel Small, Faultless Finish Editing
Proofreader: Carrie Mumford

Published by
Robert Chomany
Calgary, Alberta, Canada
bchomany@telusplanet.net

Printed in the United States of America

www.bawbsravenfeathers.net

This series of books is dedicated to my mom—without her love, patience and guidance I would not be the man I am today. She taught me to appreciate compassion, to stand alone, and to be proud of who I am, and she gave me strength to pursue my dreams.

Judge not my words, my looks, or my smile,
first put on my shoes and then walk for a mile.
I'm here in this life, to live and to grow,
so just pull up a chair and I'll share what I know.

The Moment

The moment I cried for the first time, the world knew I was alive. The moment I shared my first word, the world knew I was able to communicate. And the moment I took my first step, the world knew I was on my way to independence.

So many moments fill our lives, so many incredible events and actions, so many turning points and firsts, and we remember so many—some with great detail, some with just a smile of fondness, but we remember.

Even our childhood memories of moments seem to stay fast in our minds. We can recall our favorite toys, the TV shows we watched in black and white, and the first tree we climbed. Each memory is a moment in time, a moment we can share. We can use color and words to express the awesomeness of the events that etch a place in our consciousnesses.

As we grow, the moments of wonder occur further apart—the time seems to increase between moments of glory and bliss. The course of our journey takes us to more sedate places, where we can reflect and appreciate the footprints we have made. This is not to say that moments of incredible joy and happiness do not occur later in life. In fact, as we get older, we tend to accept more easily the things that make us happy, the things that brighten our moments. We give youth back to the young, but keep enough of it in our hearts to brighten our smiles and welcome the day. Watching a child go through their own moments is now a gift we can experience.

A moment is a marker, a reference. It is also a break in time, a bridge to a peaceful place, or a breath needed to regroup. Moments can be controlled or planned; moments can be lost or wasted; moments can be gifts of peace or love; and moments can be enjoyed by just you or with many.

Moments are energy and light; moments are fleeting and stable; moments are the ripples you see on a lake that turn into waves of emotion and then disappear, allowing serenity. The harder you try to make a moment last, the faster it is spent. The more excited you become about a moment as it approaches, the longer it takes to arrive. Such then is the uniqueness of that special moment.

Knowing the constancy of time and the unpredictability of a moment, we can live for each moment and cherish the beauty of life. We can embrace the children of today as they hold the future of our moments in their hands. And we can enjoy the simplest of pleasures, the little things that life brings—a child's smile, a friend's hug, a loved one's kiss—all the things that happen, in just a moment.

Today is filled with many moments—enjoy every single one.

One step, one page, one day at a time,
today only comes once, so let's make it shine.
You have a whole lifetime to frit away minutes,
but only one chance to enjoy life, so live it.

There should be no questions when something feels right,
    just live for the moment and hold on real tight.
    Laugh from your belly and live with no shame;
it's not all about winning if you're enjoying the game.

Maintain focus on that which you seek,
but live for today not the end of the week.
Enjoy every moment and the small things you do,
and give yourself credit if kudos are few.

Cherish the moments between planned events—
they are moments to reflect on where time is spent.

You close your eyes then surmise life will stop and wait,
but alas you find, you're left behind, still standing at the gate.
Take hold as life unfolds to everything that comes your way;
learn from living in yesterday, and live life for today.

We're given a chance to join life and have fun,
but remember in living there's more than Act One.
No scenes to rehearse, no scripts to be read,
just moments that happen, impromptu instead.
No right way, no wrong, no fault and no shame,
we all acting as humans, keeping life in the frame.

Take a moment today to just BE,
think of nothing, and set your mind free.
Listen to your breath, feel the wind on your face;
wherever you are, THAT is your space.

Live life with fervour, each moment is new.
Your story unfolds as it's written for you.

Today I know that yesterday holds
the memories of all I've seen,
locked away in that day are all the smiles
of everywhere I've been.
Today I know tomorrow will come,
and with it comes new light,
yet I live in today, for it is here
that my energy can take flight.

Light creates sparkle on the waters of time,
wind touches softly our footprints in line.
Through lifetimes of journeys our stories abound,
but where we are destined is yet to be found.
Take a moment today and cherish a thought,
for your dreams and your memories are all that you've got.

Today is where you need to be as yesterday falls behind; tomorrow's still a day away, so don't pay it any mind.

One step, one page, one day at a time,
my life unfolds along destiny's line.
I welcome each morning as it goes by so fast,
seems I barely move forward and it's already passed.
Knowing each day quickly comes to an end,
there's always enough time to make a new friend.
With each moment of life that is precious and new,
remember all those who are close to you.

Never wait to wish you had when something passes by; today is yours to live your life the best you can first try.

Solitude

Perhaps the first thing that comes to mind when you hear the word "solitude" is isolation; however, isolation is not solitude. To be at one with yourself is to be "with" yourself— focused on all your positive energy and separated from all that is negative energy. You are alone with the universe and joined with the light that is your soul.

Solitude most often is a gift, by design—one you have asked for, one you appreciate. In this day and age, actually finding the time to be alone, and I mean really alone, is hard to do. It takes planning and strength. It might mean finding the strength to turn off your cell phone and leave it at home; or if you are home and seeking solitude, it might mean turning everything off for one night. Pull the curtains closed, unplug absolutely everything electronic, and surround yourself with quiet. Listen to yourself breathe, listen to the solitude of your existence, if even for a short while.

To experience the grandeur of really being alone, one must pack up and leave the confines of society for a sleepover with nature, preferably on the side of a mountain, after a half day's hike to get there—a place where all you can smell is your own fear, which, by the way, can be detected by everything with teeth, so you might want to relax and enjoy yourself. Enjoy the feeling of one in the company of one: you.

Life does not get any better than the experience of total and absolute isolation from anything nature can not provide—concrete, steel, rubber, glass. Go ahead, hug that tree; it really can be your best friend. If no one can see the trees, does that one tree make a difference in the world? It might to you.

Solitude is the ability to be the only one in a world of billions. In your home, in your car on the way to work, enjoy every second of solitude, and eventually, you will grow to come to it naturally. Before you know it, you will be standing in a long lineup feeling very much at peace, as you will have found solitude in your mind, your "happy" place.

Wherever you may be, whatever you may be doing, whether in a group or by yourself, find that strength within to breathe, to be successful, to achieve, to be singled out, and yes, to find solitude.

Then, take your newfound strength one step further and practice escaping, just one night a month. Really work at it—lock the doors, unplug the phone, turn everything off, light a candle, reflect on all that is wonderful, and breathe . . .

So long as your soul allows life to abide,
so long as you share a smile so wide,
so long as you love your life as one only,
you will never be alone nor ever be lonely.

You are never alone so long as you are
in the company of yourself.

Escape to the serenity of a memory you keep,
somewhere safe where once you could sleep.
Nothing here is out of place,
as you've remembered exactly this time and space.
In the calm of the water a reflection you see—
the person you are, the person you'll be.

Somewhere between right and wrong is a place I know,
a place where I find peace of mind, a place I like to go.
Although I try each and every day to share my brightest smile,
sometimes it's nice to just hang out and enjoy me for a while.

It's a beautiful thing when you reach deep inside,
and all that you find is strength, honor, and pride.

Every day can be the best if you let your energy flow;
look for the happy that lives inside and watch the stresses go.

What happens when you walk where no one else has stepped?
What happens when you cry when no one else has wept?
You go to places no one has seen;
you reach new heights where no one has been.
You alone can soar in the winds to get where you need to be;
you alone can figure out the things you need to see.

To know who you are take a look deep inside;
it is there that you shine and there that you hide.
When you do find yourself to be who you are,
then the you that is shared is much better by far.

Use the eyes within your heart to see
the beauty that sets you apart.

Stand alone if you can in a forest full of trees,
a forest that's refreshed with the new morning's breeze.
Though life has been grand with the people I've known,
I am always relaxed living life on my own.

Simplicity

This could be one of the simplest things to write about, or I could analyze the heck out of it and make it complicated. Life should be simple. Every day, life is full of choices, all of which have different outcomes—the result of each choice may change or alter your current path. So if we seek to choose the simple way of life, then living becomes simpler.

Often we are faced with problems or dilemmas, but we as humans tend to lose sight of the initial cause of a situation and immediately turn to a global resolve for even the simplest problem. Yet if we step back for a moment and focus only on what happened to cause the problem, then the problem generally fixes itself—simple. We tend to inject all sorts of unnecessary components into day-to-day emotional or stressful events. The initial situation is forgotten, and the world comes to a crashing end because of something that has no relevance to anything.

Wouldn't it be nice if we had the strength to believe in ourselves and simply enjoy the simple things in life? A simple kiss just for being a kiss, a hug simply for expressing warmth and caring, a nod of approval for simply acknowledging a job well done? No reason, no cost—just simple life at its best. We all have the ability to accept the world as a simple haven of beauty, a place where energy and light is carried by winds aloft, kindness and caring is appreciated and reciprocated, and respect and honesty are a way of life—simply beautiful.

To seek the simple is to accept what is because it is; to live and let live; to give because it just feels good. This way of life is part of the soul and exists within our hearts. Emotions are created and enhanced by the choices we make. I choose to love, simply for the wonderful feelings of warmth that are shared in love. I choose not to analyze what love is or why it is—it just is: beautiful. I look at the day I am gifted with each morning and enjoy the simplicity behind it. I choose not to criticize the weather, the time, the traffic, or the cost of tea in china. Life is simply a gift. I enjoy it.

It's simple really: just believe in you—who you are and why you are. Just grasp the simplicity of life. When you make time to smell the flowers, breathe in the beauty. When you share a smile, share your energy behind it and light up the world—the simply beautiful world around you.

Enjoy the simple things in life.

Sit on the banks, watch the stream trickle by
then lay in the grass, watch the clouds in the sky.
Life should be stressless, laid back, and smooth;
ruts are too deep you should be in a groove.

Seek not the rainbow nor the gold at its end,
for that's just a fable and folklore, my friend.
The treasure you'll find at the end of the rain
is the warmth from the sun that you soon will attain.
Look for the silver in all of the clouds;
don't let your happiness be hidden by shrouds.
Life changes daily, if you blink you may miss
the beauty of simplicity or the dew's subtle kiss.

Make time to notice things in life that are real—
cherish moments of happiness and the way that you feel.

Answer life's questions as each one is posed,

using knowledge you've gained on your way.

Keep your tasks simple, and hone all your skills—

it's a sure way to lengthen your stay.

Have you ever woken up and just known who you are?
Enjoyed simply being and just felt like a star?
It's easier than you think to do this each day;
you just need to love living in every way.
No blame if you fail 'cause you gave it your all,
no worries or bother should you happen to fall.
Just get up and get on with a positive smile,
and take time to breathe every once in a while.

Flowers are beautiful, and this you can tell,
by taking a moment to see how they smell.

Have you ever tried to think a thought
and nothing came to mind?
Have you ever looked for things in life
you never seem to find?
The trick is not to look at all,
just relax and let life flow;
the simple things will come to light,
if you believe in what you know.

When you can enjoy doing nothing all day,
you've reached a place where it's easy to stay.
You just have one chance to dig what you do,
so make time when you can to take in the view.

Finding simple happiness doesn't really take much—
a smile from a friend or a subtle soft touch.
To find what you love means you ought not to look,
'cause it's found in your pet or the depths of a book.
Don't waste your time seeking things you can't see,
just love what you have and enjoy being free.

Serenity

Serenity: that moment in time where the universe that surrounds you is calm, where the wind that shares your energy is but a whisper, and ambient light blends with the light of your soul. Peace of mind is conducive to a serene life. With serenity, one can accept the wind and the rain, one can adapt to immediate surroundings and love without condition.

Nature is our teacher when it comes to the serene. There are so many beautiful images of peace in nature—happy places. The areas of serenity we travel to, to calm ourselves, can be created by visualizing the places where we are most at peace.

Serenity is balance. Balance means finding a calm spot to recover from day-to-day stresses, a place to go where you are surrounded by tranquility. Yes, it is achievable; you let stress in, so you can also let calm replace it. It is your mind after all—your will, your thoughts, your world, created by an environment of mental and physical conditions. Choose the easiest of paths and you choose the path to balanced calm.

Serenity can easily be shared by a soul full of calm energy. This energy is felt in a warm hug, a look of recognition, or a genuine smile. This sharing of balance and calm creates serenity achievable by one or one hundred. It can be felt and seen by simply believing it is real. You have the ability to share your light and energy. You can enter a room and believe the room is a calm place—and it will be. This is creating your own serenity; this is finding your own balance.

I find my serenity by soaring with my ravens, or resting on a rock ledge looking out over a vast forest of green. I get my strength from the winds and share this strength as energy in those same winds. I enjoy sharing my energy with those in my world; I look forward to creating an environment of calm in a virtual windstorm. It takes only a smile or a gesture of reassurance to return the winds to a gentle breeze. I look with anticipation to my tomorrows, as with them comes the opportunity to create new memories, to share smiles and adventures, to share my path with someone who neither follows nor leads.

Serenity surrounds us. It is in everything. It is a single raindrop or the ripples on the pool that many raindrops create. It is different for each individual yet achievable by all. It is required to maintain balance and can be the best part of every day.

Find it. Feel it. Enjoy it.

There is no way to understand
all that happens in the world;
instead just drift in gentle peace
with softened sails unfurled.
Listen then to the song of the wind,
for it shares each day anew;
it fills your life with energy—
be happy being you.

Find a cloud at which to gaze,
and revel in the sky's expanse;
take a moment to rest your mind
and your life will be enhanced.
You go hard all day at what you do,
your energy quickly depletes;
just five minutes and a walk about,
and stress you'll quickly beat.
Your wellness thrives on balance and calm,
and this you need to see:
that rest and fun go hand in hand to keep your spirit free.

I looked one day into the eyes of my dog,
    he shared with me his light.
He has no questions of why life is,
    he just sees what is right.
As long as I love him the same each day,
    he has no expectations;
imagine if humans were just as calm—
    there would be no trepidation.

Remember the story of the tortoise and hare?
It was all about the tortoise and how he fared.
It's time to step forward and speak for the rabbit,
who was doing to him what was merely a habit.

We all tend to live our lives in a hurry,
and life often passes in a mind-numbing flurry.

It's your own life, so set your own pace—

life isn't always about winning a race.

The moon is full over the frozen lake,
    its glow is silvery white.
A shadow is cast from a raven's wing
    as he soars the sky at night.
The world is still, the wind whispers a song—
    its soothing melody is carried along.

At the end of the day when the sun goes away,
it's time to release all the strife;
to recall what you've done, reflect on the fun,
and share hugs with those in your life.

Stress is when you realize there's only one of you,
and on your plate you will find a million things to do.
Hit the brakes, pull the reins, take a breath of air;
one thing at a time, my friend, will always get you there.
Only do what you can do, you are nobody's pawn.
The world still spins if you slow down, and life will just go on.

Traffic can be a time to reflect,
on yesterday's triumphs, good things you expect.
Lineups can seem like a product of fate,
but give you a chance to breathe while you wait.
In with good energy every breath that you take,
and enjoy being positive, every step that you make.

Life is given to each of us
to live as we see fit;
enjoy your day, rest when you can,
make a moment to stop and sit.
Life will go on, and when you are ready,
amble on slowly, keep your pace steady.

When do you see the beauty that surrounds?
When do you hear the music profound?
When can you feel the serenity of the wind?
When do you sense good before it rescinds?
These things come naturally if you simply believe;
start with the fondness of memories retrieved.
Then calmly drift to a warm serene place,
which sets your mind in a wonderful space.

Should you sit in the wind and listen to it sing,
your heart will feel free, and peace it will bring.
A calm will ensue from deep down inside;
you'll find balance through hope, and put fears aside.
The song of the wind is different for each,
but to all who do listen its beauty will reach.

When the mind is at peace, the soul has a rest,
all your senses are heightened, and life looks its best.
Your vision is focused on what needs to be seen,
your sleep is so peaceful and filled with new dreams.
When the mind is at peace, your days just seem brighter;
with newfound balance your light shines much whiter.

Beauty

Is it still in the eye of the beholder, or have the beholder's eyes been distracted by pixels and refresh rates? Do we still have an interest in what surrounds us? Have we lost our ability to see the colors of a sunrise? Do we no longer have the time to calmly sit and watch a pink sunset? From the hot tub outside on my deck, I have enjoyed every moment of what nature shares with me. It makes me wonder if others remember what the beauty of nature looks like.

Balance and focus, spirit and calm—all are connected to nature, should you make the time to see it. Something as simple or as simply complex as the threads of silver spun craftily into the web nestled in the corner of your deck—have you looked at it? Have you seen the amazing little creature that toiled all night to make it? Or were you rushed and instead just ran by it on your way to . . . somewhere. Do the young people of today know what nature sounds like, what beauty really means? Do we as adults take the time to show them?

I was fortunate as a lad to have a teacher who took the time to walk with me. She showed me the softness and color of a blue crocus that grew amidst a field of brown grass; she let me bond with little brown bats and carry them in my shirt pocket. We would listen to the song of hummingbirds as they hummed between flowers; and we sat on the beach and marveled at the beauty and majesty of the mountains.

My teacher was my mom. She taught me patience, taught me to care about nature and to share all of its gifts. And to this day, I don't go a day without appreciating that which nature shares. It may seem funny to some, but I am connected to nature by the trees in my yard and the wind that shares my energy. Occasionally I am given a special gift from nature: a couple of years back, I watched as a family of skunks grew and played in my backyard. They were beautiful to me.

It is so important to connect in some small way with beauty, whatever you think beauty is. You don't need to be told—everyone has a different vision, each of us has our own concept of beauty. What is important is to see it, hear it, or even feel it whenever you can, as often as you can, as it is the integral piece of the puzzle.

Beauty is a fulcrum for balance, the melody behind the song that plays in your head. Beauty is what softens the harsh environment society creates. You don't need to go far to experience it; you just need to put down the iPod and the cell phone, turn off the TV and the radio, and then walk outside, close your eyes, and breathe. It really is beautiful. Open your eyes and count the stars, or watch the clouds create shapes in the sky. Listen for the song in the wind or the happy chirping of a nearby bird. Nature in its simplest form offers its greatest beauty. Celebrate life, slow down and see beauty, find balance within you, then share your newfound calm.

When you look with your eyes, can you see with your heart?

Does beauty jump out, can you set it apart?

A flicker of light, from a dragonfly's wing,
catches your eye and makes your head swing,
    to the beauty of life that often gets lost,
to the smell of the flowers enjoyed at no cost.

The air we breathe is free for now,
beauty is ours to behold;
your ears can hear the song of the wind,
your eyes can see life unfold.

See the world for its beauty, feel the warmth of the sun;
hear the song in the wind as the river has fun.
Share the simplest of things, a smile from the heart;
life happens around you without using charts.
With growth there is happiness, with happiness there is light;
live in light, always, like the stars of the night.

The beauty of living can be seen every day,
just believe that it is real.
Use your eyes to see the wonders of life,
and use your soul to feel.

Beauty is not just in what you see,
beauty is wild and in all that is free.
Beauty is also in what you can hear,
in things that you feel and things you hold dear.
It lives in the light of a gorgeous full moon;
it's heard in the cries of a lone drifting loon.

This new day brings beauty to tall standing trees,
new colors of life for all eyes to see.

Is there a place where beauty exists without the need to see?
Of course there is—beauty exists in the hearts of you and me.

Beauty is in the laughter we share,
and felt in the sand with toes that are bare.
Beauty lives and grows in the heart,
for you to enjoy, right from the start.

Time

Do you have it? Can you afford it? Is it really something you can buy? Can it be managed? Time can be your biggest asset, or your worst enemy. It can create a relaxing moment, if you savor it, or it can turn your life into a train wreck if you waste it. The number one leading cause of health issues is stress, and the largest contributor to stress is time. If you have it, keep it. If you don't have it, you had better make it, or else you run late, you miss a connection, you are to blame—from bad to worse.

In the time it took me to write this, babies were born, their time began; people died, their time was up; and in between, lives changed for the first time, or choices were made for the last time. How versatile is time, yet, how impossible it can be to manage.

Society has even created courses you can take to learn how to manage your time. Really? Are you that busy, that programmed, that you have to learn how to manage your time so you can get more done for someone else? What about YOUR time? When do you take the time to make time for your quiet time, for your family, for you? To rest after a full day of making sure everyone else's time has benefitted from your use of it?

Society has also created things for you to practice after you have perfected how to use your time "properly." You can now learn how to unwind, how to relax, how to stretch muscles that are as tight as a steel beam—yoga, tai chi, massage therapy, reading a good book, etc. Do you see the pattern forming here? We learn how to tell time at the age of two and then it takes over our lives.

I think it's time to rethink living. It's high time, in fact, that we as human beings reconsider why we are. Our purpose, I believe, is to be—yes, just be. We need to relearn how to play, how to enjoy, how to share our time with ourselves. Understandably, we also have responsibilities: we have lives to live, families to support, etc. Working is definitely a part of life, but the key here is to keep it just a part. Life is filled with moments—moments that turn into memories, moments that can be cherished. The moment it takes to share a hug or a simple smile can turn a second of time into a beautiful day.

Remember to live to your fullest extent as our time on this planet is short. Make the time to enjoy, take the time to love everything. Why not? It doesn't cost you anything to have, or to share, feelings, and it only takes a heartbeat to enjoy living.

Life happens once and passes fast;
keep your eye on tomorrow and cherish the past.

To and fro and back again
>   we try to reach a goal;
the drive is there and the energy—
>   we feel it in our souls.
Then in a flash, the day is gone,
>   no hope in getting it back,
but alas we've managed to forget to do,
>   with such an awesome knack.
At the end of the day if you did your best
>   and just smiled as you tried,
you'll feel the calm that comes along
>   with gratitude and pride.

Time waits for no one, and tomorrow always comes;
just in time for a few of us and way too soon for some.
We greet each morning with open arms and really have no say;
life just happens all the time as destiny has its way.
Take a minute on this new day to enjoy just being you.
Sing, dance, grab the wind, smell a flower or two.

Have some fun and grow a bit, let troubles pass you by.
Tomorrow's on its way you know, with another chance to fly.

Monday comes, Sunday is gone,
the time it passes true;
don't hurry life as then you'll find
you've missed a chance or two.
Share a smile or smell a rose,
see a bird in flight;
relax your pace, slow down your race,
take time to live life right.

Don't rush your life just let it be;
things will happen quite naturally.
Time is a constant, it tends to just flow,
for some of us quickly, for others it's slow.
Life is what happens between plans that you make,
so enjoy the whole journey with each step that you take.

Good things come to those who wait,
no matter how much may be on your plate.
Life is your book, you write every page;
as time passes, you write like a sage.

We do all we can to make our life grand,
yet waste precious moments exalting the bland.
Enjoy what you see, pay no mind what you've missed;
life happens quickly— beautiful sunrise, soft kiss.
Cherish the moments and squeeze out the best,
love from your heart, and live life with zest.

I will continue to soar with my Raven spirit,
and I will continue to share with you his feathers of wisdom.
I find great joy in sending smiles in the wind
and in hugging others with the warmth of my words.

Acknowledgments

I would like to thank the people in my life who have been there to help me along this new and uncharted path on which I walk.

Rachel Small - Editor, Faultless Finish Editing
Carrie Mumford - Proofreader
Jessee Wise - Illustrator
Fiona Raven - Designer

And to the souls in my life who have given me strength, support and inspiration, this adventure would not have happened without you all.
Special thanks to Meeho, my brother, my friend.

About the Author

Robert (BawB) Chomany is the author of the BawB's Raven Feathers series, pure and simple inspirational books. He was born in Calgary, Alberta, with a clear view of the mountains to the west. These mountains eventually drew Bob in, and he spent many years living in the company of nature, exploring his spiritual side.

Bob pursues his many interests with passion. You are just as likely to find him twisting a wrench, or riding his motorcycle, as you are to find him holding a pen, writing.

Bob still lives in Calgary, where he finds happiness by simply living with a smile and sharing his words of wisdom with others.

www.ingramcontent.com/pod-product-compliance
Lightning Source LLC
Chambersburg PA
CBHW032047290426
44110CB00012B/984